The Secret Garden

FRANCES HODGSON BURNETT

Level 2

Retold by Anne Collins
Series Editors: Andy Hopkins and Jocelyn Potter

Pearson Education Limited
Edinburgh Gate, Harlow,
Essex CM20 2JE, England
and Associated Companies throughout the world.

ISBN 0 582 42659 6

This edition first published 2000

NEW EDITION

Copyright © Penguin Books Ltd 2000
Illustrations by Annabel Large
Cover design by Bender Richardson White

Typeset by Pantek Arts, Maidstone, Kent
Set in 11/14pt Bembo
Printed in Denmark by Norhaven A/S, Viborg

Published by Pearson Education Limited in association with
Penguin Books Ltd, both companies being subsidiaries of Pearson Plc

For a complete list of the titles available in the Penguin Readers series please write to your local
Pearson Education office or to: Marketing Department, Penguin Longman Publishing,
5 Bentinck Street, London W1M 5RN.

Contents

Introduction

'That tree's in the secret garden,' Mary thought. 'Oh, I'd like to fly over the wall and see the garden!'

She looked carefully at the wall again. But she couldn't see a door anywhere.

Mary Lennox is ugly and cross and she is often ill. When she is nine years old, her parents die. Mary goes to live with her uncle. He lives in a big, old house in the country. There are gardens round the house. One day, Mary finds a secret garden. It has walls round it, and she cannot find a door. For the first time in her life, Mary is interested in something. She wants to go into the secret garden.

Mary meets two boys, Dickon and Colin. Dickon is poor but happy, and he loves animals. Colin is rich, but ill. He thinks he is going to die.

What is the secret of the secret garden? Will Mary get in there? How does the garden change the lives of Mary, Colin and Dickon?

Frances Hodgson Burnett was born in 1849 in Manchester, England. Her father died when she was four. In 1865, when Frances was sixteen, the Hodgson family moved to America. The family was poor, so Frances wrote stories for newspapers and magazines. In 1873 she married Dr Swan Burnett. She wrote one very famous book, *Little Lord Fauntleroy*, in 1886.

Frances Hodgson Burnett wrote more than forty books. She wrote her most famous book, *The Secret Garden*, in 1911. Nearly 100 years later, children everywhere read and enjoy this story of an unhappy boy and girl and a magical 'secret' garden. Frances Hodgson Burnett died in 1924.

Chapter 1 'Where is Everybody?'

Mary Lennox had a thin little face and always looked cross. Nobody liked her and she was often ill. Mary's parents were English, but they lived in India. Mr Lennox worked there. Mrs Lennox was very beautiful and had many friends. But she did not like children. So when she had a baby, Mary, she was not interested in her. Mr Lennox had a lot of work and was not at home very often. Mrs Lennox gave the baby to an Indian servant.

'You take the child,' she said to the servant. 'I don't want to see it or hear it.'

The thin, ugly baby grew into a thin, ugly little girl. When the little girl wanted something, the servants gave it to her. They never said 'no' because they didn't want her to cry. When she cried, Mrs Lennox was angry.

So, at the age of six, Mary was not a nice child. Nobody loved Mary and Mary loved nobody.

One hot morning, when Mary was nine years old, a new servant woke her. 'Where's *my* servant?' Mary shouted.

The woman looked afraid. 'She can't come,' she said.

She left the room, and nobody came into Mary's room all morning. It was very strange.

Mary did not know it, but people in the house were very ill. That day, her servant died, and three more servants died the next day. Mary stayed in her room and everybody forgot about her. Sometimes she cried, and sometimes she slept. She went into the dining-room and ate some food. Then she found some wine and drank it. It made her sleepy.

She went to her room again and slept for a long time. When she woke, the house was very quiet. 'Why doesn't anybody come and see me?' thought Mary.

But nobody came. Then she heard voices outside. 'It's very sad,' a man said. 'That pretty woman! And the child too!'

A man and a woman came into Mary's room. She was near the window and she looked sad and ugly.

'There's a child here! Who is she?' cried the man.

'I'm Mary Lennox,' the little girl said angrily. 'I was asleep and I woke up. Where is everybody? Where's my servant?'

The man looked at her sadly. 'Little girl,' he said, 'your parents died two days ago. And the servants ran away.'

'Everybody forgot me,' thought Mary. 'Everybody.'

Chapter 2   Mary Goes to England

For a short time, Mary stayed with friends of her parents, Mr and Mrs Crawford. Their children did not like her.

'You're going to go to England,' the oldest boy said to Mary. 'My parents told me. You're going to live with your uncle. He lives in a house in the country. He's a hunchback.'

Mary felt afraid when she heard this. That evening, Mrs Crawford talked to her. 'You're going to go to England, my dear,' she said. 'You're going to live with your uncle, Mr Archibald Craven, in Yorkshire.'

'Where's Yorkshire?' asked Mary.

'In the north-east of England,' answered Mrs Crawford.

She went to Mary and put her arms round her. But the child pulled away from her. 'She's an ugly little thing,' Mrs Crawford thought.

◆

Mary went to England with an English family. In London, one of Mr Craven's servants met her. The servant's name was Mrs Medlock. She was a fat woman with a red face and small black eyes. Mary did not like her and she did not like Mary.

They caught a train to Yorkshire. Mary sat quietly and looked out of the window. She felt very unhappy.

'My mother and father didn't want me,' she thought. 'The Indian servants didn't like me. Nobody likes me.'

Nobody said to Mary, 'People don't like you because you aren't nice.' So she didn't understand.

It was a long journey to Yorkshire. Mrs Medlock got bored and started to talk. 'Mr Craven's house in Yorkshire is a strange place,' she said. 'It's 600 years old and it's in the middle of the country. There are 100 rooms, but we don't use many of them. There are big gardens round the house and tall old trees.'

Mary said nothing.

Mrs Medlock tried again. 'Mr Craven won't see you much. He's a strange man. He's not interested in anybody. He's a hunchback. When he was young, he was very unhappy. Then he married and he changed.'

Mary started to feel interested, and Mrs Medlock saw this. 'Mr Craven's wife was a kind, pretty woman,' she said. 'He loved her very much. When she died– '

'Oh! Did she die?' Mary asked.

'Yes,' Mrs Medlock answered. 'And Mr Craven got stranger and stranger. He's often away now. He doesn't see people. When he's at the house, he stays in his rooms. So you won't see him. When you're in the house, *you'll* have to stay in *your* rooms. But you can play in the gardens.'

Mary turned her face to the window and did not speak. After some time, she slept.

When she woke, it was dark. The train was at a station.

'Let's go!' cried Mrs Medlock. 'We're here. Be quick! We have to drive to the house.'

They drove through a small town, then out into the country. It was dark and Mary could not see much.

'It's 600 years old and it's in the middle of the country.'

'We're going to drive across the moor,' said Mrs Medlock.

'What's a "moor"?' asked Mary.

'We'll be on the moor in a minute, and then you'll see.'

The horses started to climb higher. Now there were no trees and it was very dark. 'Nothing grows on the moor, only grass and flowers,' said Mrs Medlock.

After some time, they stopped in front of a very large house. They went inside into a big, dark room with pictures of people on the walls. Mary looked very small in her black coat. A thin, old man came and spoke to them. He was Mr Craven's servant.

'Mr Craven doesn't want to see her,' he said. 'He's going to London in the morning.'

'All right, Mr Pitcher,' Mrs Medlock said. 'Come with me, child.'

She took Mary to her bedroom. There was a fire in the room and dinner on the table.

'Here you are,' Mrs Medlock said. 'This room and the next room are yours. You have to stay in them. Don't forget that!'

Then she left. The little girl sat down and ate. She felt unhappy and very afraid.

Chapter 3   Martha

When Mary woke the next morning, there was a servant in the room. The child sat up and looked out of the window. It was very strange. There were no trees, only red-blue grass.

'What's that?' she asked the servant.

'That's the moor,' answered the girl. 'Do you like it?'

'No,' said Mary. 'I hate it.'

'That's because you don't know it,' the servant girl answered. 'I love it. In the spring and summer there are flowers everywhere. It's very beautiful.'

'What's your name?' asked Mary.

'Martha Sowerby,' said the girl.

'You're a strange servant,' Mary said. Martha was very different from the servants in India. Indian servants did not speak much.

Martha laughed. She had a round face and she looked kind.

'Are you going to be my servant?' Mary asked.

'I'll help you sometimes,' said Martha.

'Who's going to dress me?' asked Mary.

Martha opened her eyes very wide. 'Can't you put your clothes on?' she asked.

'No,' said Mary crossly. 'My Indian servant always dressed me.'

'You'll have to learn,' said Martha.

Mary suddenly felt very angry and unhappy. She started to cry.

'Don't cry!' Martha said. 'Please don't cry.' Her voice was kind and Mary stopped crying.

'I'll bring you your clothes and help you with them,' Martha said. She went to a cupboard and took some clothes out. There was a white dress and a white coat.

'These aren't mine,' Mary said. 'Mine are all black.'

'Mr Craven doesn't want you to wear black clothes,' said Martha. She helped Mary with her clothes. The child put out her hands and feet and did not move.

'Can't you put on your shoes?' asked Martha.

'No, my servant did that,' said Mary.

Martha laughed and began to talk about her family. 'There are twelve of us,' she said. 'And my father doesn't make much money. Sometimes there isn't much food in the house. But the children love playing on the moor. My mother says that they eat the grass! My brother Dickon, he's twelve years old, and he's got a young horse!'

'Where did he get it?' Mary asked.

'He found it on the moor when it was a baby,' answered Martha. 'They're friends now. It follows him everywhere. Dickon's a kind boy and animals like him.'

'I always wanted an animal,' Mary thought. She began to feel interested in Dickon. This was very strange. Mary was never interested in other people.

'Come and have your breakfast,' said Martha. There was a big breakfast on the table in the next room. But Mary never ate much and she did not want to eat now.

'I don't want any food,' she said.

'But it's very good!' said Martha. 'My brothers and sisters are always hungry.'

'I'm never hungry,' said Mary. But she drank some tea and ate a little bread and butter.

'Now go outside and play in the garden,' said Martha. 'Perhaps you'll want your food when you come in.'

Mary went to the window and looked out. It was winter. Everything looked cold and grey. 'It's too cold,' she said.

'What are you going to do inside?' asked Martha.

Mary looked round the room. There was nothing there for children.

'All right, I'll go outside,' she said. 'But who'll come with me?'

'Nobody,' said Martha. 'You'll be all right. Dickon goes out on the moor and plays for hours. Nobody goes with him. The birds come and eat bread from his hand.'

This interested Mary. 'I'll go outside and look at the birds,' she thought. 'They'll be different from the birds in India.'

Martha took her downstairs. 'Go through that door and you'll find the gardens,' she said. 'But you can't go into one of the gardens. Mr Craven closed it ten years ago and nobody can go in there.'

'Why not?' asked Mary.

'He closed it when his wife died,' Martha answered. 'She died very suddenly. It was her garden. He threw away the key to the door. Oh! Mrs Medlock's calling me. I have to go!'

Chapter 4   Ben Weatherstaff and the Robin

Mary went outside and started walking through the gardens. They were very big and there were many trees and plants. But it was winter and there were no flowers. The place did not look very pretty.

The child thought about Martha's words. 'Mr Craven loved his wife,' she thought. 'So why did he throw away the key to his wife's garden? Why can't people go in there? It's very strange. It's a *secret* garden. I'd like to find it!'

She stopped and looked round. On the right, there was a high wall. There was a green door in the wall, and Mary walked through it, into another garden. This garden had walls all round it. There was an old man with a spade in his hands.

'What is this place?' Mary asked him.

'It's a kitchen garden,' the gardener answered. He did not look very friendly.

'What's a kitchen garden?' asked Mary.

'A garden with fruit and vegetables for the kitchen,' he answered crossly.

'Do kitchen gardens always have walls round them?' asked Mary.

'Yes,' said the old man.

Mary walked through three more kitchen gardens. She came out into the big gardens again and looked round. There was another wall on the left. 'Another kitchen garden!' she thought, and she looked for a door. But long plants grew down the wall and she could not see one.

'That's strange!' she thought. 'There are trees on the other side of the wall. So there's a garden there, but no door into it.'

There was a bird in the tallest tree and he started to sing. Mary stopped and listened to him. He was a pretty little red and brown bird and his song was pretty too.

'He's calling to me,' Mary thought. After a short time, the bird flew away. 'I think the bird was on a tree in the secret garden,' she thought. 'Perhaps he lives there and knows all about it.'

She walked back into the first kitchen garden and found the old man.

'There's one kitchen garden with no door into it,' Mary said. 'There are trees on the other side of the wall and I saw a little red and brown bird in a tree there. He sang to me.'

The old man laughed and looked friendlier. Suddenly, the little red and brown bird flew into the garden. He came and stood on the ground near the old man.

'Hello, my little friend,' laughed the man. The bird put his head on one side and looked at them. He was very pretty.

'What is he?' Mary asked.

'Don't you know? He's a robin. Robins are the friendliest birds in the world. He knows that we're talking about him. Look at him.' The old man laughed again.

'Where's his family?' Mary asked.

'He hasn't got a family,' the man answered.

'*I* haven't got a family,' Mary said quietly.

The old gardener looked at her for a minute. 'Are you the little girl from India?' he asked.

'Yes,' Mary answered.

'They told me about you,' he said.

'What's your name?' asked Mary.

'Ben Weatherstaff,' the old man answered. '*I* haven't got a family. The robin's my only friend.'

'I haven't got any friends,' said Mary. 'People don't like me and I don't like them.'

'We're the same, you and I,' said Ben Weatherstaff. 'We aren't very nice.'

'Am I really as unfriendly as this old man?' thought Mary. She didn't like the idea. The robin flew to a tree and began to sing. 'Why's he doing that?' Mary asked.

'He wants to be your friend,' the old man answered.

Mary walked to the tree and looked up.

'Do you really want to be my friend?' she asked the robin.

'You said that very nicely!' cried Ben Weatherstaff. 'Perhaps you *are* a child and not a cross old woman. Dickon talks to the birds too.'

'Do you know Dickon?' Mary asked.

'Everybody knows him. Dickon goes everywhere.'

Mary wanted to ask more questions about Dickon. But suddenly the robin flew out of the tree and over the wall.

'Oh!' Mary cried. 'He's flying into the garden with no door!'

'He lives there,' said Ben. 'In a rose-tree.'

'Rose-trees!' said Mary. 'Are there rose-trees there?'

Ben Weatherstaff turned away from her. 'That was ten years ago,' he said.

'I'd like to see them,' said Mary. 'Where's the door? I know that there *is* a door.'

Ben Weatherstaff looked angry. 'There was a door ten years ago, but there isn't one now,' he said. 'Now go away. I have to work.' And he walked away.

Chapter 5   Somebody is Crying

For the first weeks in Mary's new home, every day was the same. Each morning, Martha made the fire and brought Mary her breakfast. The child got bored when she stayed in the house. So she went outside and played in the gardens every day. She did not know it, but this was the best thing for her. She began to look stronger.

One morning she felt hungry and ate all her breakfast.

'Breakfast is nice today,' she said to Martha.

'You're hungry because you play outside,' said Martha.

'I don't *play* in the gardens,' said Mary. 'There are only trees and plants there. I can't *play* with them.'

'You can look at them,' said Martha. 'My brothers and sisters look at things.'

So Mary looked at the trees and the plants and the birds. She often went to the wall of the secret garden. Plants grew all over the wall and she was interested in them. One day she saw the robin again. He was on top of the wall.

'Oh,' she cried, 'is it you − is it you?'

The robin began to sing. Mary thought, 'He's talking to me. He's saying, "Good morning! Isn't everything nice?"'

'I like you,' she cried. Suddenly, the robin flew away and sat in a tree on the other side of the wall.

'That tree's in the secret garden,' Mary thought. 'Oh, I'd like to fly over the wall and see the garden!' She looked carefully at the wall again. But she couldn't see a door anywhere.

That evening, she asked Martha, 'Why does Mr Craven hate the garden?'

'I'll tell you,' Martha said. 'But don't talk about it to anybody.'

'I won't,' said Mary.

'Mrs Craven loved that garden, and only she and Mr Craven went in there,' Martha said. 'There was a big, old tree in the garden. Mrs Craven often sat in it and read. One day she fell out of the tree. She died the next day. After that, Mr Craven didn't see anybody for months. He closed the garden and he threw away the key to the door. Now nobody can go in there. He doesn't want us to talk about it.'

'That's very sad,' said Mary.

Suddenly she sat up and listened. She could hear the sound of the wind outside, but there was another sound inside the house. 'Is somebody crying?' she asked Martha.

'No, no,' said Martha quickly. 'It's the wind.'

'But listen,' said Mary. 'It's *inside* the house. A child's crying.'

She listened again. The sound was quite loud now. 'Yes, I'm right,' said Mary. 'A child's crying.'

The door to her room was open. Martha ran to it and shut it. The sound stopped. 'It was the wind,' Martha said.

But Mary looked at her and thought, 'No, it wasn't the wind. But who is it? Who's crying?'

◆

The next morning, Mary looked out of the window. 'It's raining,' she said. 'What am I going to do? I can't go out.'

'Why don't you read?' said Martha.

'I haven't got any books,' Mary answered.

'There's one room in the house with a lot of books,' Martha said. 'I'll take you there tomorrow.'

Mary didn't answer. Martha left the room and, after a short time, Mary left her room too.

'I'm going to find that room now,' she thought. 'Mrs Medlock says that there are 100 rooms. I want to see them!'

She walked through many large rooms, but she did not see any books. Suddenly she stopped. 'I can hear that sound again,' she thought. 'Somebody *is* crying. It's coming from that room there.'

She went to the door and put her hand on it. Suddenly, it opened and there stood Mrs Medlock. 'What are you doing here?' the servant said angrily.

'I'm sorry,' said Mary. 'But somebody's crying.'

'Nobody's crying,' said Mrs Medlock. 'Go back to your room!' She walked with Mary to her room and pushed the child inside. 'Now stay there,' she said. 'I'm going to find a teacher for you. *I* haven't got time for you.'

Mary sat down in front of the fire. She was very angry, but she didn't cry. 'I was right!' she thought.

Chapter 6   The Secret Garden

Two days later, the weather changed. Mary woke up and went to the window. 'Look at the moor!' she cried to Martha. The sky was blue, and the moor looked very beautiful.

'Yes, it's nearly spring,' said Martha.

'I'd like to see your house, Martha,' Mary said.

'I'll ask my mother,' said Martha. 'She'd like to meet you.'

'I don't know your mother, but I like her,' Mary said. 'And I don't know Dickon, but I like him too.'

'You'll meet Dickon one day. Do you think he'll like you?' Martha asked.

'No,' said Mary in a cold, little voice. 'People never like me.'

'And do *you* like Mary?' Martha asked.

Mary thought for a minute. 'No, I don't think I do,' she said.

That morning, Mary felt sad and cross. She went outside and began to feel better. She went into the first kitchen garden and found Ben Weatherstaff there. 'Spring's coming,' he said. 'Things are growing. You watch!'

'I will,' said Mary.

She looked round and saw the robin. He put his head on one side and looked up at her. 'Do you think he remembers me?' she asked.

'Of course he remembers you!' cried Ben Weatherstaff. 'He wants to know you.'

'Are things growing in *his* garden?' Mary asked.

'What garden?' Ben asked crossly.

'The garden with the rose-trees,' Mary answered.

'Ask him,' said Ben. 'He knows.'

Mary said goodbye to the old man and walked slowly through the gardens to the wall of the secret garden.

'I like the secret garden and the robin,' she thought. 'And I don't know Dickon or his mother, but I like them. And Martha is

kind. I never liked people in India and now I like four people.'
(For Mary, the robin was a person.)

Then the most wonderful thing happened – and it was because of the robin. She looked round and there he was on the ground near her. 'You followed me!' she cried. She sat on the ground and put her hand out. The robin did not run away. 'I'm happy!' Mary thought.

Suddenly, she saw something on the ground near the robin. It was an old key. 'Perhaps it's the key to the secret garden!' she thought. She took the key back to her room and looked at it for a long time.

The next morning, Mary took the key and went to the wall of the secret garden. The robin was on top of the wall.

She laughed. 'You showed me the key yesterday. Perhaps you'll show me the door today,' she said.

Then something magical happened. There was a strong wind that day, and suddenly it moved the plants under the robin to one side. Mary looked – and there in the wall was a door. 'The door to the secret garden!' she cried.

She felt very excited. She took the key from her coat and put it in the door. It was not easy, but slowly she turned the key. She pushed the door and it opened. She walked through and quickly shut the door behind her. She looked round excitedly. She was *inside* the secret garden!

It was very early spring, and there were no flowers. But there were rose-trees everywhere, and rose-plants climbed over the walls and the other trees in the garden. 'It's the strangest, place in the world!' Mary thought.

The grass was brown, everything was brown. 'Is anything growing here? Everything looks very dead,' she thought.

Mary walked round the garden. There were little green plants in the ground. She looked at them carefully. There was grass round them and the plants couldn't grow very well. She started to pull up the grass round the plants. 'That's better,' she said.

She took the key from her coat and put it in the door.

She worked busily all morning. At midday, she went back to the house. 'I'll come back this afternoon,' she thought.

Mary ate a lot of lunch and she looked well and happy. Martha saw this and smiled.

After lunch, Mary said, 'Martha, I'd like a spade.'

'Why?' Martha asked.

'I'd like to make a little garden. I want to plant seeds. I want to grow things. How much does a spade cost?'

'Not much,' answered Martha.

'I've got some money,' Mary said.

Martha thought for a minute. 'I know,' she said. 'Why don't you write a letter to Dickon? He can buy you a spade and some seeds. He can bring them to you.'

'That's a good idea!' cried Mary.

So that afternoon she wrote a letter to Dickon. She felt very excited. 'I'm going to meet Dickon!' she thought. 'And I'm going to plant seeds and they'll grow. The secret garden will be green and beautiful again!'

Chapter 7   Dickon

It was sunny all week, and Mary went to the secret garden every day. She loved being outside in the sun and the wind. She didn't look ill now – she looked well and happy. Every day there were more little green plants. She pulled up the grass round the plants. 'I love doing this!' she thought. 'I'm happy here!'

She often talked to Ben Weatherstaff. He was friendlier now, and he told her about the plants in the gardens. One day, Mary was in one of the kitchen gardens. She heard a sound and turned round. There was a boy under a tree and round him there were little birds and animals.

The boy smiled at her. 'I'm Dickon,' he said, 'and you're

Miss Mary.' He was about twelve years old. He had blue eyes and a friendly smile. 'I've got your spade and seeds,' he said.

'Let's sit down and look at them,' Mary said.

The two children sat down on the grass and Dickon told her about the seeds. Suddenly he stopped. 'I can hear a robin,' he said. 'He's calling to us. Where is he?'

'He's in that tree,' Mary answered. 'He's Ben Weatherstaff's robin, but he knows me too.'

Dickon listened carefully to the robin's song. 'Yes, he does,' he said, 'and he likes you.'

'Do you understand the birds when they sing?' asked Mary.

'*I* think I do. And *they* think I do!' Dickon said. Then he asked, 'Where's your garden? I'll plant the seeds with you.'

Mary said nothing. Her face went red, then white. After a minute or two, she said slowly, 'I don't know you. But I'm going to tell you a secret. Please don't tell anybody.'

'I never tell secrets,' said Dickon.

'Listen!' Mary said quickly. 'I found a garden! It isn't mine. Nobody wants it, nobody goes there – only me.'

'Where is it?' Dickon asked quietly.

'I'll show you,' Mary answered. She got up and he followed her to the secret garden wall. She put her hand under the plants and there was the door. 'This is it,' Mary said. 'It's a secret garden, and only you and I know about it.'

Dickon did not speak for two or three minutes. Then he said quietly, 'It's a strange place. But it's very pretty! The garden's sleeping. I always wanted to see this place,' he said.

'Did you know about it?' asked Mary.

'Speak quietly!' said Dickon. 'We don't want people to hear us. Yes, Martha told me about it.'

'Will there be roses in summer?' Mary asked. 'Or are they all dead?'

'Yes, there'll be roses,' Dickon said. 'Look!'

He went to a rose-tree and took a knife from his jacket. He cut some wood from the tree and showed it to Mary. 'Look!' he said. 'This is old wood here, but this green wood is new.'

'Oh, good!' cried Mary. 'I want everything to be green and beautiful!'

'Let's go round the garden and cut away the old wood,' said Dickon. 'Then the new wood can grow.'

They worked hard for some time.

'The garden will be fine,' said Dickon. He looked at some little green plants in the ground. 'Who pulled up the grass round those plants?' he asked.

'I did,' said Mary. 'They didn't look very happy, so I helped them.'

'You were right. They'll grow beautifully now.'

'I love gardening,' cried Mary. 'I'm getting stronger and I'm not tired.'

'I love gardening too,' said Dickon. He stopped and looked round him. 'There's a lot more work here,' he said.

'Will you come again and help me?' Mary asked him.

'I'll come every day,' Dickon answered. 'We'll wake up this garden and make it beautiful!'

'Dickon,' said Mary, 'Martha says that you're nice. And you *are* nice. I like you. I never liked people before.'

Dickon laughed. 'People think I'm strange. But you're *really* strange!' he said.

Mary was quiet for a minute. Then she asked, 'Do you like me?'

'Yes, I do,' Dickon answered. 'And the robin likes you too. We like you very much.'

They worked in the garden for another hour. Mary felt very, very happy. At lunchtime, she went back to the house, but Dickon stayed in the garden. 'I'll come back after lunch,' Mary said.

Chapter 8   Mary Meets Mr Craven

Martha was in the room when Mary got back.

'I met Dickon!' Mary told her.

'And do you like him?' asked Martha.

'I think – I think he's beautiful,' Mary said.

Martha laughed. 'Dickon isn't *beautiful*,' she said.

'*I* think he is,' said Mary.

She ate quickly because she wanted to go back to Dickon. But Martha said, 'Mr Craven's here. He wants to see you.'

Mary's face went white. 'Perhaps Mr Craven will go into the secret garden,' she thought. 'He'll know that I was in there!'

'Why does he want to see me?' she asked. 'He didn't want to see me when I first came here.'

'It's all right,' said Martha. 'He's going away again tomorrow.'

Then Mrs Medlock came in and took Mary to Mr Craven's rooms. He was in a chair by a big fire. 'Come here!' he said.

Mary went to him. She looked ugly and cross again. But she looked at her uncle carefully. His back was not very bad. He was not really a hunchback, but he looked very sad.

'Are they good to you?' he asked her.

'Yes,' she answered.

'You're very thin,' he said.

'I'm getting fatter,' Mary said coldly.

'Do you want a teacher?' Mr Craven asked.

'Oh, please, I don't want a teacher, not now!' cried Mary. 'I want to play outside. But I would like one thing. Can I – can I have a very small part of the gardens?'

'Why?' asked Mr Craven.

'I want to plant seeds and grow things,' Mary answered. She felt very afraid. 'Perhaps he'll say no,' she thought.

'Do you like gardens very much?' Mr Craven said slowly.

'Yes, I do,' said Mary.

Mr Craven got up and walked across the room. 'Yes, you can have a small part of the garden,' he said. 'Make it green and beautiful.' He looked very tired now. 'Go now, child,' he said. 'Goodbye. I'll be away all summer.'

Chapter 9 'I'm Colin Craven'

That night, it rained heavily. Mary woke up and could not sleep again. Suddenly, she sat up in bed. 'It's that sound again!' she thought.

She left her room and walked through the dark house. Sometimes she stopped and listened. She came to a door with a light under it. 'The sound's coming from here,' she thought. 'And I met Mrs Medlock here before!'

Slowly she opened the door. She saw a room with a large bed in it. There was a boy in the bed. He was about ten years old and he had a thin, white face and big, grey eyes. He did not see Mary and she watched him for a short time. He cried and then stopped. Then he cried again. He looked tired and ill.

Mary walked into the room. The boy turned and saw her. 'Who are you?' he asked. He looked very afraid.

'I'm Mary Lennox,' the little girl answered. 'Mr Craven's my uncle.'

'He's my father,' said the boy. 'I'm Colin Craven.'

'Your father!' cried Mary. 'I didn't know about you!'

'Come here,' said Colin. Mary went and stood near his bed. 'Where did you come from?' he asked.

'My room,' said Mary. 'My parents died and I live here now. Didn't they tell you about me?'

'No,' Colin answered. 'They know that I don't want to see people. And I don't like people seeing me.'

'Why not?' asked Mary.

'Come here,' said Colin. Mary went and stood near his bed.

The boy did not speak for a minute. Then he said, 'Because I'm going to be a hunchback. So I don't want people to see me. I'm ill and I never leave this room. I get too tired.'

'Oh, this is a strange house,' said Mary quietly.

She looked round the room. There were pictures on the walls. One picture showed a young woman with large, grey eyes. There was a happy smile on her face.

'Who's that pretty woman?' Mary asked.

'That's my mother,' Colin said. 'She died when I was born. They say that I've got her eyes.'

'Does your father come and see you?' Mary asked.

'Sometimes. Usually when I'm asleep. He doesn't want to see me. When he sees me, he thinks of my mother. I think he hates me,' the boy said angrily.

'He hates the garden because she died there,' Mary said.

'What garden?' the boy asked.

'Oh – a kitchen garden,' Mary said quickly. 'Your father closed it when your mother died. He threw away the key to the door.'

Colin looked interested. He began to ask questions about the garden. 'What do the servants say about it?' he asked.

'The servants don't talk about it,' said Mary. 'Your father doesn't want them to talk about it.'

'They'll talk to me,' Colin said. 'Or I'll be angry. And when I'm angry, I get ill. When I want something, I get it. I'm Mr Craven's son.' He stopped, then he said sadly, 'But nobody thinks I'm going to live very long.'

'Do *you* think you won't live?' asked Mary.

'Yes,' Colin answered coldly.

'Do you want to live?' asked Mary.

'No,' he answered crossly. 'But I don't want to die. When I feel ill, I think about my back. Then I cry and cry. But let's not talk about it. Let's talk about the garden. I want the servants to find the key. I want them to take me there.'

'Oh, don't – don't – don't do that!' Mary cried.

'Why? You want to see the garden too,' said Colin.

'We don't want other people to find the garden!' Mary cried. '*We* want to find the garden – then it will be *our* garden – our *secret* garden.'

Colin began to understand. 'Secrets are nice,' he said.

There was a wheelchair in the room. Mary looked at it and thought for a minute. Then she said slowly, 'Perhaps we can find a boy, and he can push your wheelchair. We can go to the garden and nobody will know.' She stopped suddenly. 'Mrs Medlock will be angry with me,' she said.

'Why?' asked Colin.

'She didn't want me to know about you.'

'Mrs Medlock is only a servant,' Colin said. 'I'll speak to her and she won't be angry with you. I like you!'

'And I like you,' Mary answered.

'I want you to be a secret too,' said Colin. 'I'll only tell Martha about you. She'll tell you when I want to see you.'

'Does Martha know about you?' asked Mary.

'Yes,' said Colin.

The children talked for a long time. Mary told him about her life in India and Colin was very interested. But he began to look tired.

'Close your eyes and I'll sing to you,' Mary said. She began to sing an old Indian song. Colin's eyes closed, and in five minutes he was asleep. Mary went back to her room.

Chapter 10   Martha is Afraid

The next day, the weather was bad and Mary could not go outside. When Martha came in, Mary said, 'I know about Colin.'

'Oh no!' Martha cried. 'How?'

'I heard sounds in the night. I followed them to Colin's room.'

'Oh Mary,' cried Martha. 'I didn't tell you about him, but they'll be angry with me. They'll send me away!'

'No, they won't,' said Mary. 'Colin liked me.'

'Colin doesn't like anybody!' Martha cried.

Mary laughed. 'He wants me to come and talk to him every day. He's not going to tell Mrs Medlock. It will be our secret. He'll tell you when he wants to see me. But what's wrong with him?' she asked.

'Nobody really knows,' said Martha. 'After his wife died, Mr Craven didn't want to see the baby. He said, "The child won't live. Or he'll live, but he'll be a hunchback."'

'Is Colin really going to be a hunchback?' Mary said.

'No, he isn't,' Martha answered. 'But his back's weak. A London doctor came and saw him two years ago. I was in the room when he saw Colin. He said, "My boy, there's nothing wrong with your back. Go and play outside. Then your back will get strong." But it didn't help Colin. He thinks he's a hunchback. And he thinks he's going to die.'

'Do *you* think he'll die?' asked Mary.

'I don't know. He never goes out and that's not good for him. When they took him into the garden, he got very ill,' Martha answered slowly.

She left the room, but she came back half an hour later. 'Colin wants to see you,' she said.

'I'll come now!' said Mary. She walked quietly through the house to Colin's room.

'Come in,' said Colin.

'Colin,' said Mary, 'Martha's afraid. She says they'll send her away. But *she* didn't tell me about you!'

'Bring her here,' said Colin.

Mary found Martha and brought her to Colin's room.

'They won't send you away because *I* don't want you to go.

And *I'm* Mr Craven's son. So don't be afraid. Now go away!' Colin said.

'Yes, sir,' said Martha and she left the room.

Mary said nothing for a minute. Then she said, 'You're not very nice to people! You're very different from Dickon.'

'Who's Dickon?' asked Colin.

'Martha's brother,' Mary said. 'He's twelve. He goes out on the moor a lot. He talks to the animals and birds there.'

'I can't go on the moor,' said Colin sadly.

'Why not?' asked Mary.

'Because I'm too ill. I'm going to die.'

'Who says that?' Mary asked.

'Everybody. The servants, my doctor.'

'Is that the doctor from London?'

'No, *my* doctor. He lives near here.'

'*I* like the doctor from London,' said Mary. 'Martha told me about him. He doesn't think you're going to die.'

'My father does,' said Colin. 'He wants me to die.'

'Oh no, he doesn't,' said Mary. 'But let's not talk about that. Let's talk about nice things.'

So the two children talked about Dickon and the secret garden and Ben Weatherstaff's robin. Suddenly, Mrs Medlock and Colin's doctor walked into the room.

'What are you doing here?' cried Mrs Medlock to Mary.

And the doctor cried, 'What's this? Are you all right, Colin?'

But Colin wasn't afraid of them. 'Of course I'm all right,' he said. 'This is Mary Lennox. Nobody told her about me. She found me. I want her to come and see me every day.'

'Colin, I don't think this is good for you,' the doctor said.

'Yes, it is,' said Colin. 'I feel better when Mary's here.'

The doctor looked carefully at the boy. 'All right, but don't talk for too long, or you'll get tired!' he said. And he left the room with Mrs Medlock.

Chapter 11 'I'm Going to Die!'

It rained all week. Mary couldn't go outside, so she saw Colin every day. They talked about many things. But Mary didn't tell Colin about the secret garden. 'I'll tell him when I know him better,' she thought. Then one day she said to him, 'I know you don't like meeting people. But would you like to meet Dickon?'

'Oh yes!' cried Colin.

The next day Mary woke early. The sky was blue again and it was a beautiful day. She ran outside, to the secret garden.

Dickon was there before her. 'You're here early!' Mary cried.

Dickon laughed. 'I got up before the sun,' he said.

After a week of rain, the garden was very green. The children ran round the garden and looked at the new plants and flowers. Suddenly, Dickon said, 'Look, there's the robin!'

They sat on the grass and watched him. There was a very old tree in the garden. It was bigger than the other trees. The robin flew to the tree and started to sing. 'That's the tree!' Mary thought suddenly. 'Do you think Mrs Craven fell from that tree?' she asked.

'Yes,' said Dickon. The two children were quiet for a time.

'Do you know about Colin?' Mary suddenly asked.

'Why? What do *you* know about him?' asked Dickon.

'Colin and I are friends,' Mary said. 'He likes me.'

'Yes, I know about Colin,' Dickon said. 'He's a hunchback.'

'He isn't,' said Mary. 'But he thinks he's *going* to be a hunchback. It's very sad. He never goes out.'

'I know,' said Dickon. 'Look round the garden, Mary. It's getting greener and greener.'

Mary looked round slowly. 'You're right!' she said. 'It's beautiful. What are you thinking?'

'I'm thinking I'd like to meet Colin. Then we can bring him here. I think he'll feel better here.'

'Yes!' cried Mary. 'I think he will too. I'll tell him about our garden. I don't think he'll tell anybody.'

The two children worked in the garden all morning. Then Mary went into the house for lunch.

'Colin wants to see you,' Martha told her.

'I'll see him later this afternoon,' answered Mary.

'He'll be angry with you,' Martha said.

But Mary ran outside. 'Dickon's waiting for me,' she cried.

It was early evening when she came back inside. Martha did not look happy. 'Colin's very angry because you didn't go to see him,' she said.

Mary felt cross. She liked Colin, but he was not as important as the garden or Dickon. But she went to see him.

He was in bed. 'Why didn't you come?' he asked.

'I was in the garden with Dickon,' Mary said coldly.

'That boy isn't going to come here again,' Colin said angrily.

'Then I won't come here again!' Mary cried.

'Oh yes, you will!'

'No, I won't!'

'You unkind girl! I'm ill and I'm going to die!'

'No, you're not!' cried Mary.

Colin sat up when he heard that. 'You know I am!' he cried.

'No you're not, you stupid boy!' shouted Mary.

Colin threw a book at her. 'Get out of here!' he cried.

Now Mary felt really angry. 'I'm going and I'm not coming back!' she cried.

She ran out of the room. When she got back to her bedroom, she found some books on the table. They were from Mr Craven. There were some picture books and two books about gardens.

'That's kind of Mr Craven,' she thought. 'He remembered me.' She suddenly felt happy. Then she remembered Colin. 'He thinks he's going to be a hunchback,' she thought. 'He's very unhappy. Perhaps I *will* go and see him tomorrow.'

The two children worked in the garden all morning.

She was tired, so she went to bed early. But in the middle of the night, she woke up. 'What's that noise?' she thought. Then she understood. 'It's Colin. He's crying really loudly.' She felt angry. 'Can't somebody stop him?' she thought.

Martha came into her room. 'Oh Mary!' she cried. 'It's Colin. Nobody can do anything with him. He likes you. Can you come and talk to him?'

Mary ran to Colin's room. She opened the door and ran to the bed. 'Stop it!' she shouted. 'I hate you! Everybody hates you! Why don't you die, you stupid thing!'

'I can't stop!' Colin cried. 'I can't!'

'Yes, you can,' shouted Mary.

'I'm going to be a hunchback!' Colin cried. 'I know I am! I felt my back and it's different.'

'Don't be stupid! Show it to me.'

'All right. You'll see!' Colin cried. He showed Mary his back. The girl looked at it carefully. His back was thin and weak but there was nothing wrong with it.

'You're not going to be a hunchback,' said Mary loudly. 'Your back is as good as mine.'

Colin smiled weakly. 'Really? Is it really all right?'

'Yes!'

Colin turned to Martha. 'Do you think I'll live?' he asked.

'Yes!' said Martha. 'But you have to go outside. You have to run and play, Colin. Then you'll be fine.'

'Then I'll go with Mary,' the boy said quietly. He felt happy suddenly. 'I'm all right!' he thought. 'I'm all right!'

'Now sleep,' said Mary. 'Would you like me to sing to you?'

'Yes,' he said.

Mary took his hand and sang to him. Colin slept.

Chapter 12   Mary Tells Colin the Secret

It was a lovely day when Mary woke the next morning. She wanted to go outside, but she went to Colin's room.

'You came!' he cried. He looked very tired. Mary sat down and they talked about Dickon and his animals and birds.

'Can Dickon really talk to animals?' Colin asked.

'*I* think he can,' Mary answered. 'He says everybody can. But you have to be friends with the animals first.'

'I'd like to have friends,' Colin said sadly. 'But I don't like people.'

'Don't you like me?' Mary asked him.

'Yes, I do,' Colin answered.

'Ben Weatherstaff says that he and I are the same. We're not very nice to people. Perhaps you're the same,' said Mary. She thought for a minute. 'But I think I'm nicer now.'

'Mary,' Colin said quietly, 'I was unkind about Dickon yesterday and I'm sorry. I hated him because you liked him. But I was wrong. I want to meet him.'

'Good,' Mary answered, 'because he wants to meet you. Perhaps he can come and see you tomorrow.' She took Colin's hands. 'Colin,' she said slowly, 'I'm going to tell you a secret. Please don't tell anybody.'

'No, no, I won't,' Colin answered.

'Listen. I found the door to the secret garden – and I found the key too,' Mary said quietly.

'Oh Mary! Can I see it? Will you take me there?'

'Yes,' answered Mary. 'And Dickon will push your wheelchair.' She talked to him about the secret garden for a long time.

Later that day, Colin's doctor visited him with Mrs Medlock. 'So you were ill last night, my boy,' he said.

'Yes, but I'm better now,' Colin answered. 'I'm going to go outside and see the gardens.'

The doctor did not look happy. 'Be careful,' he said.

'Mary's going to come with me,' said Colin. 'And Dickon will push my wheelchair.'

'Oh, Dickon!' said the doctor. 'You'll be all right with Dickon.'

He left the room with Mrs Medlock. 'I saw Susan Sowerby, Dickon's mother, last week,' Mrs Medlock said. 'I told her about Mary and Colin. Susan said, "Children have to be with other children. Mary will be good for Colin." Perhaps she's right.'

'Yes, perhaps she is right,' said the doctor.

Colin slept well that night. The next morning Mary ran into the room. 'Dickon's coming!' she cried excitedly.

The door opened and Dickon came in. There was a bird on his arm. Colin's mouth fell open.

'Will it sit on my arm?' cried Colin.

Dickon laughed. 'You have to be friends with it,' he said.

The two boys talked all morning. They looked at pictures of plants and flowers.

'These flowers are in the secret garden,' Dickon said. 'And these.'

'I'm going to see them!' cried Colin. Dickon smiled.

Chapter 13   Colin Sees the Secret Garden

The next day was sunny and warm. Colin spoke to Mrs Medlock. 'I'm going outside. I don't want to see anybody in the gardens.'

'Yes, sir,' Mrs Medlock answered.

A servant carried Colin downstairs and put him in his wheelchair outside the house.

'You can go now,' Colin said.

The servant went back inside. Dickon pushed Colin's wheelchair, and Mary walked next to them. They saw nobody in the gardens. But they walked round for a long time before they went into the secret garden.

'This – this is the door! Push the wheelchair inside quickly, Dickon!' Mary cried.

Inside the garden, Colin looked round and said nothing for some minutes. Everything was green now and there were flowers everywhere. The sun was warm on Colin's thin face. 'Oh,' he cried, 'it's beautiful! I'm going to get well!'

That afternoon, Colin laughed and talked. He began to feel better. Dickon and Mary worked with their spades, and Colin sat under a fruit tree in his wheelchair.

'That's a very old tree over there,' Colin said suddenly.

'Yes,' said Dickon quietly. He did not want to talk about it. Suddenly the robin flew into the garden. 'Look, there's the robin!' Dickon cried.

'Where?' asked Colin. He looked up and saw the little bird. Then he laughed and forgot about the tree.

Mary looked at the robin and thought, 'There's magic in this garden. I know there is. The magic sent the robin. Colin won't think about the tree now.'

'I'm going to come here every day,' Colin said.

'Yes,' said Dickon. 'In a short time, you'll walk and use a spade too.'

'Walk!' said Colin. 'Use a spade! Will I?'

'Yes,' said Dickon. 'You've got legs. You have to make them strong.'

Colin smiled. Mary thought, 'I think Dickon makes magic. He's going to make magic for Colin, and Colin will get better.'

It was nearly evening and the garden was very quiet. Suddenly Colin cried, 'Who's that man?'

Mary and Dickon turned round and there was Ben Weatherstaff. They could see his head over the top of the wall. The old man looked very angry. He could not see Colin and Dickon, only Mary.

'How did you get into the garden, you bad girl?' he shouted.

'The robin showed me the door,' Mary answered.

'Take me there,' Colin said to Dickon.

Dickon pushed the wheelchair nearer Ben Weatherstaff. When Ben saw Colin, his mouth fell open.

'Do you know me?' Colin asked him.

'Yes, you're Mr Craven's son,' Ben answered slowly. 'How did you get in here? You're a hunchback!'

'I'm not a hunchback!' Colin said loudly.

'No, he's not!' Mary shouted. 'I saw his back and it's fine.'

'Help me, I want to stand,' Colin said to Dickon. Dickon took Colin's arm, and slowly the boy stood up. He looked thin but very tall. 'Now – look at me, Ben Weatherstaff!' he cried. 'Am I a hunchback?'

For a minute Ben could not speak. Then he said, 'No, you're not a hunchback. You're very thin, but you're fine.'

'Come into the garden,' Colin cried. 'Mary will open the door.'

'Yes, sir,' said Ben, and he climbed down from the wall.

'Dickon!' Colin said, 'I'm going to walk to that tree.' With his hand on Dickon's arm, the boy walked slowly to the tree. When Ben came through the door, Colin cried, 'Look! Am I a hunchback?'

'No, you're not,' the old man said again.

'Listen!' the boy said. 'This garden's a secret. Don't tell anybody about it. You can come sometimes and help.'

'Thank you,' Ben Weatherstaff said, and he smiled.

Chapter 14   The Magic in the Garden

When Colin went back into the house, his doctor visited him. 'You were outside too long,' he said.

'But I'm not tired,' answered Colin. 'I feel better and tomorrow I'm going to stay outside all day.'

The doctor did not look happy about this.

After he left the room, Mary said, 'You aren't very nice to your doctor.'

Colin thought about this. 'You're right,' he said. 'I can be very unkind to people. I'll try to be nicer.'

'Good,' said Mary. 'The garden will help you. I think there's magic in the garden. You'll be happy there and you'll learn to be kind.'

◆

That spring and summer there really was magic in the garden. It grew more and more beautiful. There were flowers of all colours and the roses climbed everywhere.

'Your mother loved those flowers,' Ben Wetherstaff told Colin.

The children went to the garden nearly every day. Dickon often brought his animals and birds, and the children played with them. Colin grew stronger and happier. One day he took a spade and he started to dig. He only worked for five minutes. But each day he worked for a longer time. One afternoon he walked round the garden. Dickon and Mary walked next to him and the robin sang in a tree.

'The magic is making me strong!' Colin cried. 'I'm not going to tell the doctor,' he said. 'I'll only tell him when I can run really well. And when my father comes home, I'll walk into his room. I'll say, "Here I am. I'm very well and I'm going to be a strong, happy man."'

Mary laughed. 'I can't wait!' she cried.

There was only one problem. Because Colin was often outside, he was always hungry.

'I'm eating more now,' he told Mary. 'The servants will know I'm getting better.'

◆

Dickon told his mother about the secret garden and Colin. She was very interested and asked a lot of questions. He told her about Colin's problem with food.

34

One afternoon he walked round the garden. Dickon and Mary walked next to him.

Mrs Sowerby laughed. 'I've got an idea,' she said. 'Colin and Mary can give me money. Then I'll give you food for them.'

It was a wonderful idea. Each day Dickon came with bread, cake and milk. The food was good and they all ate it. After that, Colin did not want to eat much in the house.

His doctor could not understand it. 'It's strange,' he said to Mrs Medlock. 'The boy isn't eating, but he's getting fatter!'

'You're looking much stronger', he said to Colin. 'Your father will be very happy when he hears about this,' said the doctor.

'No, don't tell him!' cried Colin. 'I'll get ill again!'

'All right,' said the doctor quickly. 'We won't tell him.'

When he left, Colin looked at the picture of his mother.

'I never wanted to look at her picture before,' he told Mary. 'But now I like it. I think she wants me to be happy.'

Mary looked at the picture. 'Yes, I think she does.'

◆

The three children and Ben were in the secret garden one morning, when suddenly the door opened. A woman with a very kind face stood there. She smiled at the children.

'Who is it?' Colin cried.

Dickon ran across the grass.

'It's mother!' he shouted. 'You wanted to meet her, so I told her about the secret garden.'

Colin went to Mrs Sowerby. 'Hello, Mrs Sowerby,' he said. His eyes were very big in his face.

'Oh, dear boy!' Mrs Sowerby said.

'Do you think my father will like me?' Colin asked her. 'I'm strong and well now, but perhaps he won't like me.'

'Of course he will,' Mrs Sowerby answered. She turned to Mary. 'You're a pretty girl, Mary,' she said. Mary laughed.

The children took Mrs Sowerby round the garden. Colin and Mary did not know Dickon's mother, but they loved her. She had food. They sat down under the trees and ate. The children told her about the magic in the garden.

'Of course there's magic here,' said Mrs Sowerby. 'But I have a different name for it. For me, it's plants and trees and flowers. It's green things – it's life!'

At the end of a happy morning, Colin said quietly, 'When do you think my father will come home, Mrs Sowerby?'

'I don't think it will be long, Colin,' she answered.

Colin looked at her with love in his eyes. 'I'd like you to be my mother,' he said.

Mrs Sowerby took him in her arms. 'Your mother's here. I know she is,' she said. 'And your father will come back to you.'

Chapter 15   In the Garden

When you think sad or unkind things, it is bad for you. In India, Mary did not like people – she did not like anything! So she was ill and cross. Then she came to Yorkshire. There she thought about secret gardens and robins, about Dickon and the moor. She was a pretty child now, and she was nicer and happier.

It was the same with Colin. Before he met Mary, he thought only about his back. But now he thought about his new friends and the secret garden. He thought about happy things and so he was a happy person.

Colin's father, Archibald Craven, was away all spring and summer. He visited the most beautiful places in Europe. Nothing helped him. He thought only of his dead wife.

One day, he was in the Austrian mountains. He was tired and he sat down on the grass. There were blue flowers everywhere and it was very quiet. He looked at the flowers for a long, long time. Everything got quieter and quieter. 'Something is happening to me,' he thought. 'What is it? I feel – I feel happy again!'

That night, he slept for a long time. In his sleep, he heard his dead wife's voice. 'Archie, Archie!' she said.

'Where are you, my dear?' he asked.

'In the garden,' she answered, 'in the garden.'

When he woke the next morning, it was a beautiful day. 'In the garden,' he thought. 'She said, "In the garden." But I threw away the key!'

A servant came in with a letter. It was from Susan Sowerby. She wrote: 'Please come home, Mr Craven. It's very important. Your wife would like you to come home.'

Mr Craven read the letter carefully. 'I will go back,' he thought. 'I'll leave today.'

On the journey back to Yorkshire, he thought about Colin. 'I'm a bad father,' he thought. 'My son is ten years old. But is it too late? Can I help him?'

When he arrived at the house, Mrs Medlock came to see him. His first question was, 'How's Colin?'

'He's . . . he's different.' Mrs Medlock answered slowly. 'It's very strange. He's fatter, but he doesn't eat much. He goes out into the gardens every day in his chair. Miss Mary and Susan Sowerby's boy take him.'

'Where is he now?' Mr Craven asked.

'In the garden, sir. He's always in the garden.'

Mrs Medlock left the room and Mr Craven repeated the words again and again: 'In the garden!'

He went out into the gardens and walked slowly through them. 'Where's the key?' he thought. 'I threw it away. I can find the door, but can I find the key?'

He came to the secret garden wall and found the door. Then he stopped and listened. He could hear voices inside the garden! But why? Nobody went into this garden!

Suddenly the door opened and a boy and a girl ran out. The boy ran out very fast. He didn't see Mr Craven, and he ran into his arms. Mr Craven looked at him. He was a tall boy with dark hair and big, grey eyes.

'Who – what – who?' cried Mr Craven.

'Father, I'm Colin,' the boy said.

For a minute his father could not speak. Then he said quietly, 'In the garden, in the garden!'

'Yes,' Colin said quickly. 'I'm better because of the garden. And because of Mary and Dickon and the magic. Nobody knows I'm better. I wanted you to know first.'

Again, Mr Craven could not speak. His son was happy and well! This was the best thing in the world!

'I'm well and I'm going to live, father!' Colin cried.

Mr Craven took his son's arm. 'Take me into the garden,' he said.

So Colin took him in. It was autumn now, and there were autumn colours everywhere. Roses climbed over the trees and the walls.

'It's beautiful!' cried Mr Craven. 'But why? I shut the garden ten years ago. Why isn't everything dead?'

They sat down on the grass, and Colin told his father the story of the secret garden. He told him about the robin, Ben Weatherstaff, the animals and the magic. Then he said, 'I don't want it to be a secret any more. I'm never going to get into that chair again. I'll walk back to the house with you, father.'

And he did. Ben Weatherstaff was at a window and he called the other servants. 'Look!' he said. 'Who do you think is coming across the grass?'

The servants ran to the windows. Mrs Medlock threw up her hands. 'Oh!' she cried. 'It's not possible!'

A tall, strong boy came across the grass. There was a happy smile on his face. It was Colin Craven!

ACTIVITIES

Chapters 1–5

Before you read

1 Find these words in your dictionary. The words are all in the story. Then answer the questions.

grass   hunchback   key   moor   plant   robin   rose   servant spade

    a Which are words for people?

    b Which things do you find in a garden?

    c What do you find in a door?

    d Which is a word for a place?

2 What do the words in *italics* mean? Look in your dictionary.

    a He arrived an hour *ago*.

    b She's always *cross* with me about something.

    c I put things in a *secret* place under my bed.

    d Which *side* of the street do you live on?

    e He has a very loud *voice*.

3 Why do you think the secret garden is a secret? How can a garden change children's lives?

After you read

4 What do you know about these people and things?

    a Mary Lennox   **d** Martha   **g** Ben Weatherstaff

    b Mr Craven   **e** Mrs Medlock

    c Mr Craven's house **f** the secret garden

5 Work with another student. Have the first conversation between Mary and Ben.

    Student A: You are Mary. Ask about kitchen gardens, the robin, Dickon and the rose-trees on the other side of the wall.

    Student B: You are Ben Weatherstaff. Answer Mary's questions.

Chapters 6–10

Before you read

6 How can Mary get into the secret garden? Who do you think is crying?

7 Find these words in a dictionary. Put them in the sentences.

dig/dug grow magic part seed wheelchair

  a She is in a ….. because she can't walk.
  b He ….. in the ground and found a key.
  c This flower is from a ….. .
  d Do oranges ….. in your country?
  e DisneyWorld is a ….. place.
  f Which ….. of the story do you like best?

After you read

  8 Answer these questions:

  a How does Mary get into the secret garden? How does the robin help her? What does she find in the secret garden?
  b Who does Mary meet in the gardens? Where do they go?
  c What does Mary ask Mr Craven for?
  d How is Mary changing?

  9 Work with another student. Talk about Dickon, Colin and Mr Craven. Which people do you like in the story? Which people don't you like? Why? Who would you like to meet? Why?

Chapters 11–15

Before you read

10 What do you think will happen to Colin? How do you think the story will end?

After you read

11 Answer these questions:

  a What happens in the middle of the night?
  b Where do Dickon and Mary take Colin? Why do they do this?
  c Colin changes in these chapters. Why doesn't he want anybody to know about this?
  d How are Colin's mother and Mrs Sowerby important to the story?
  e Why does Mr Craven come back?
  f Why does Mrs Medlock cry, 'It's not possible!'?

12 Work with another student. Talk about these questions:

How do Colin and Mary change in these chapters? Who changes the most? Why do they change? Do you think there is magic in the secret garden?

Writing

13 In the last chapter, Colin tells his father the story of the secret garden. Write their conversation.

14 Did you know a 'magical' place when you were young? Write about it. Why did you like it?

15 In Chapter 6, Mary writes a letter to Dickon. She asks him for a spade and some seeds. Write her letter.

16 Who do you think is the most important person in the story? Why?

Answers for the Activities in this book are published in our free resource packs for teachers, the Penguin Readers Factsheets, or available on a separate sheet. Please write to your local Pearson Education office or to: Marketing Department, Penguin Longman Publishing, 5 Bentinck Street, London W1M 5RN.